# GLOVES, MITTS & PADS

## MARY ELIZABETH SALZMANN

### Consulting Editor, Diane Craig, M.A./Reading Specialist

A Division of ABDO

**ABDO**
Publishing Company

# visit us at www.abdopublishing.com

Published by ABDO Publishing Company, a division of ABDO, P.O. Box 398166, Minneapolis, Minnesota 55439. Copyright © 2012 by Abdo Consulting Group, Inc. International copyrights reserved in all countries. No part of this book may be reproduced in any form without written permission from the publisher. SandCastle™ is a trademark and logo of ABDO Publishing Company.

Printed in the United States of America, North Mankato, Minnesota
062011
092011

 PRINTED ON RECYCLED PAPER

Editor: Katherine Hengel
Content Developer: Nancy Tuminelly
Design and Production: Anders Hanson
Image research: Stacy Nesbitt
Photo Credits: Thinkstock (Jupiter Images), Shutterstock, PhotoDisc

Library of Congress Cataloging-in-Publication Data
Salzmann, Mary Elizabeth, 1968-
  Gloves, mitts & pads / Mary Elizabeth Salzmann.
    p. cm. -- (Sports gear)
  ISBN 978-1-61714-825-5
  1. Sporting goods--Juvenile literature. I. Title.
  GV745.S35 2012
  688.7´6--dc22
                        2010053049

## SANDCASTLE™ LEVEL: TRANSITIONAL

SandCastle™ books are created by a team of professional educators, reading specialists, and content developers around five essential components—phonemic awareness, phonics, vocabulary, text comprehension, and fluency—to assist young readers as they develop reading skills and strategies and increase their general knowledge. All books are written, reviewed, and leveled for guided reading, early reading intervention, and Accelerated Reader® programs for use in shared, guided, and independent reading and writing activities to support a balanced approach to literacy instruction. The SandCastle™ series has four levels that correspond to early literacy development. The levels are provided to help teachers and parents select appropriate books for young readers.

Emerging Readers
(no flags)

Beginning Readers
(1 flag)

Transitional Readers
(2 flags)

Fluent Readers
(3 flags)

# CONTENTS

# What Are...

# GLOVES, MITTS & PADS ?

Gloves, mitts, and pads are sports gear.

4

Gloves and mitts **protect** the hands.
Pads protect the body.

# BASEBALL GLOVE

POCKET

WEB

HEEL

Baseball players wear gloves.

Infielders use small gloves.
Outfield gloves are bigger.

# FIRST BASEMAN'S MITT

First basemen wear mitts. Mitts are like mittens. The fingers are together!

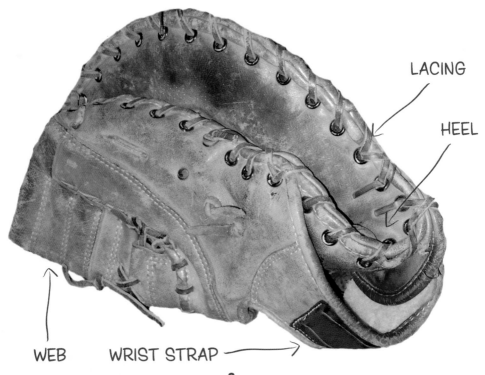

LACING

HEEL

WEB

WRIST STRAP

First basemen's mitts are big.
This helps them reach more balls.

# CATCHER'S MITT & PADS

A catcher's glove is called a mitt.

WEB

Catcher's mitts have thick padding.

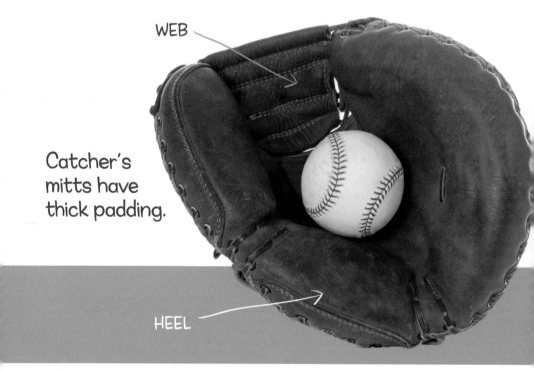

HEEL

Catchers wear pads. The pads **protect** their bodies and legs.

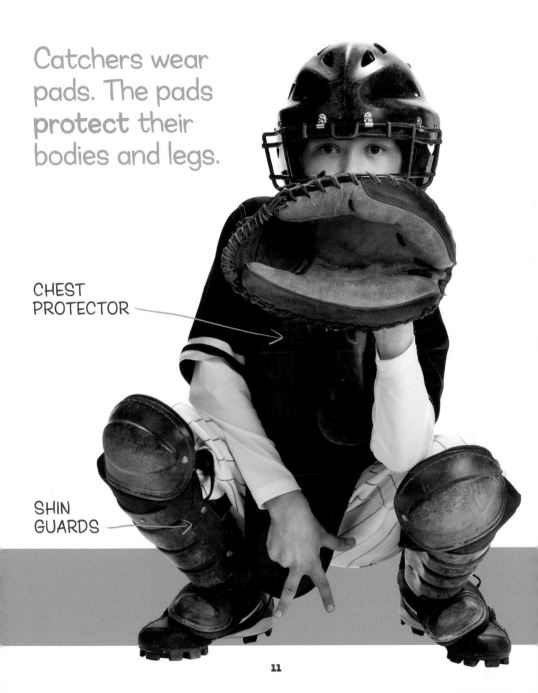

CHEST
PROTECTOR

SHIN
GUARDS

# ICE HOCKEY GOALIE'S GEAR

Ice hockey **goalies** wear two different gloves.

BLOCKER     TRAPPER

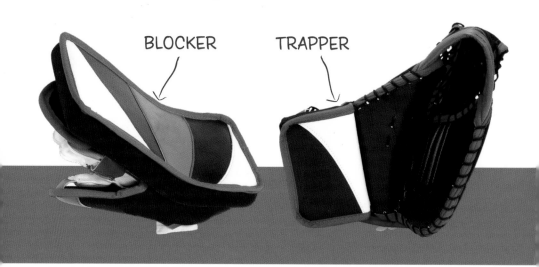

# Ice hockey **goalies** also wear pads.

Some pads are under their shirts. Others are on their legs.

CHEST
PROTECTOR

HOCKEY
GOALIE PADS

# SOCCER GOALIE'S GLOVES

Soccer **goalies** wear gloves.

Goalie's gloves have **stiff** fingers.

The gloves help the **goalie**
**grip** the ball.

# BOXING GLOVES

LACES

Some boxing gloves have laces. Others have **Velcro** straps.

VELCRO

Boxing gloves **protect** boxers' hands.

# FOOTBALL PADS

Football players wear shoulder pads.

SOFT PADDING

HARD PLASTIC

The shoulder pads go under their shirts.

Football players also wear pads
on their legs.

# SKATEBOARDING PADS

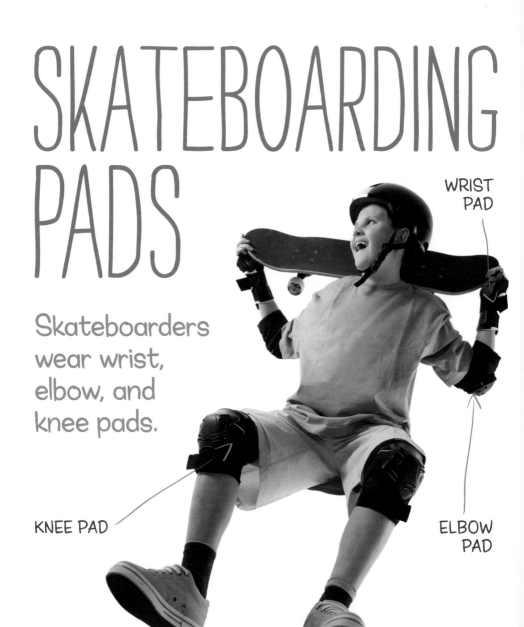

Skateboarders wear wrist, elbow, and knee pads.

WRIST PAD

KNEE PAD

ELBOW PAD

The pads **protect** skateboarders
if they fall.

# FUN FACTS

- Some baseball gloves have two thumb holes. They can be worn on either hand.

- Boxers used to tie leather around their hands. They didn't wear gloves!

- Skateboards were invented in the 1950s.

# QUICK QUIZ

1. Outfielders use small gloves. True or False?

2. Ice hockey **goalies** wear two different gloves. True or False?

3. Soccer goalie's gloves have **stiff** fingers. True or False?

4. Football pads are worn over the player's jersey. True or False?

# GLOSSARY

**goalie** – the player who guards the goal to keep the other team from scoring.

**grip** – to hold onto.

**protect** – to guard someone or something from harm or danger.

**stiff** – hard to bend.

**strap** – a strip of leather or cloth used to hold something closed.

**Velcro** – the brand name of a type of fabric that has two sides that stick together.